mDecks Series

Piano Technique Vol. 1

Fingers Control, Independence, Balance & Strength
Rhythmic Subdivisions and Essential Polyrhythms

Finger Repetitions
X Against Y

Ariel J. Ramos

Introduction

Piano Technique... So much has been said about it. So many books have been written on the hows and whys of Piano Technique that it would be of no use to attempt writing a new book on this topic. This is why *Piano Technique Vol. 1.: Finger Control Independence, Balance & Strength* is just about **practice**.

This books has 46 technical exercises for developing and maintain your technique to its best possible shape. Some exercises are for the very beginner while others require a higher level of proficiency. Exercises way above your current level are not recommended since they are harmful to your technique development. It is always advisable to have your teacher decide which level of exercises you can undertake with confidence. Piano technique involves so many subtleties that there is no substitute for a good teacher when it comes to showing the student how to do certain movements and how to feel them.

As a rule of thumb: Good piano technique is about relaxation, minimum effort and optimization of movement. In the end any **master** perform his/her art **effortlessly** and that, should always be the goal in any discipline.

In the beginning every action seems odd, out of place, every note feels alien and out of control. With practice, one tries to translate **will** into **action**, with practice one **learns what actions are feasible and consequently what to aim for**.

If you have read the *How to use the mDecks Series Books...* chapter you are ready to start.

Think... **Relaxation. Optimization. Effortless Performance. Consistency in your practice.**

Have a great practice!

The Concept behind

mDecks explained.

All the books in the mDecks series have been designed based on the same idea: **a system of "eternals vs. hierarchical challenges".**

Each exercise you practice should have a goal. These goals are sometimes hard to conquer, and finding a path that leads to them is not always easy. Frequently, we cannot decide if we are ready for the next step or if we should keep practicing the same exercise over and over again. usually forgetting the reason we started playing it. On of the reasons this is so confusing is that some exercises are meant to resolve an issue in our playing while others are a workout for our mind and body. The first ones should be played only until the issue is resolved, the latter should be part of your routine repeatedly. That's where our concept of **"eternals vs. hierarchical"** comes into play.

How to use this book

Piano Technique Vol. 1, consists of 46 exercises, covering two main technical challenges for the piano player:

- *Fingers Control Independence, Balance & Strength*
- *Rhythmic Subdivisions and Essential Polyrhythms*

Your practice and the book structure

The exercises in this book are organized in a two page layout. Left pages contain the description, and pertinent information for the exercise. Right pages contain the score, for that same exercise, in standard musical notation.

Every exercise has an unique identifier called **mDeck-cid** which, as you will see later, is very useful for your practice routine's organization and effectiveness. Also, each exercise has a **link** to its **recommended previous exercise** in difficulty. If the exercise has the *infinite* icon then is an *eternal* (meaning you can practice it any time you want, just as a workout). Otherwise, it would be an issue you need to resolve in order to reach a certain goal, in which case; and once you've mastered it., you need not practice it any further.

Two methods of practicing

- You can go in order page by page. (*eternals* can be retaken in cycles)

- Choose any page randomly or look for a topic you would like to practice, and try the exercise. If it is too challenging or seems impossible, follow the links to the previous level exercises, until you have reached the one at your current level, and then work your way up the exercise ladder to attain the desire goal. With eternals, levels of complexity exist but all levels give you a good workout.

Exercise Presentation

The graph below shows how the exercise are presented. The layout is exactly the same for all exercises. This will save you time, since you will know where and what to look for, every time you start a new exercise.

Page Content:
Eternal icon: It will be displayed only if the exercise is an eternal
Clock: with suggested time duration for the exercise
Keyboard Graph: Showing the hand position or the exercise
Link to the previous ex: If you can't play the current one, try that one.
Code for downloading an mp3 version of the exercise from mDecks.com
A link to pages at the beginning of the book with more info n the exercise
All text in italics are common to many exercises (to save you time)
An inspirational quote of the exercise. To keep you going!

This page layout will always be on the left pages of the book. Right pages will show the actual music notation of the corresponding exercise.

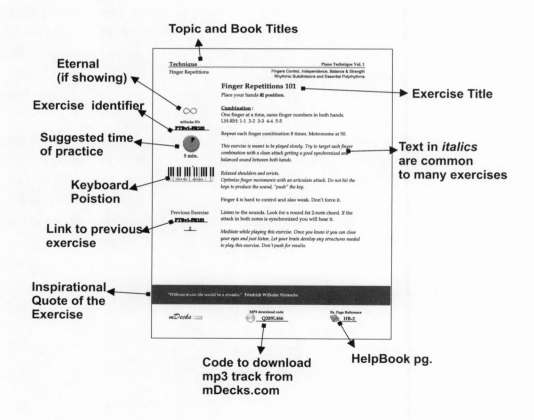

Consistency and Time

Playing the piano (or any other instrument) requires the use of very fine motor skills or dexterity. To acquire such skill, the brain must be challenged **consistently** and **repeatedly** by the same proposals, leading to a self induced auto-restructuring. This transformation is not a trivial one and it only comes to be after all the necessary work has been done and enough time has passed.

It's all about consistency and time.

Practice consistently and allow enough time for the brain to adjust. Consistency makes the challenges persist, which tells the brain a change is needed in order to solve them. Even when you are resting your brain will assemble new structures to handle those needs that your consistent practice routine has created. *Practice every day. It is better to practice 5 minutes every day than 5 hours once a week.*

Don't forget that it takes time for those structures to become functional. Sometimes your playing will seem to worsen or you will hit a wall. Don't get frustrated, allow your brain enough time to find a way around that wall, if you keep practicing, that will eventually happen and you will be cruising into your next challenge. *Do your part, practicing every day, and your brain will find its own solutions.*

Organizing your Practice routine

Any practice routine must be consistent, organized and must evaluate progress. Probably the most common reason any practice routine fails, is the lack of organization. You must know how many topics you're practicing how often, how much time per session each, where you have improve and where your areas of weakness are. Always take your time to write down all pertinent information for each exercise or topic you have practiced.

A good record keeping system is essential for your practice routine to success.

Buy a notebook or get a workbook for musicians like the one mDecks offers with 52 assignment sheets for musicians base on an organizing system of four topics a week that will last you for the entire year called:

*52 **Weeks of Practice.***

Finger Repetitions

The finger reps. exercises in this book are done in one of the following fix positions: **C position, F#7 position and Bb pentatonic F inversion position.** These positions are clearly shown in each exercise page in the keyboard diagrams.

To perform these exercises:
  • Place your hands in the correct position.

  • Push the keys, in all 10 fingers, at the same time and hold them down (it's your choice to produce sound or not when you do this)
  • Set-up the metronome at an appropriate speed (50 bmp is a good tempo for reps).

These exercises are meant to be played slowly. Try to target each finger combination with a clean attack getting a good synchronized, balanced and round sound in both hands.

  • Start the reps combination, with both hands playing at the same time, using the fingers combination as indicated. All other fingers must remain still, holding their keys down.

  • Only move the current fingers, lifting and then playing…lifting and then playing... 8x

Relaxed shoulders and wrists. Avoid involuntary movements. Analyze your playing, look at your hands. Optimize finger movements with an articulate attack. Do not hit the keys to produce the sound, "push" the key.

All these exercises are *eternals*, you can practice them forever! They will keep your fingers in shape and will maintain your dexterity intact when it comes to targeting the right finger without disturbing any of the others.

Meditate while playing these exercises. Once you know them you can close your eyes and just listen. Try to become one with the metronome, as if you were actually playing it. Let your brain develop any structures needed to play with ease. And never push for results.

Rhythmic subds. & essential polyrhythms

Polyrhythm is the simultaneous performance of two or more independent rhythms. Polyrhythms are constantly used in piano music. Piano players are basically playing polyrhythms all the time. It might be as simple as 2 notes on the right hand and one on the left. Some people correctly call this a subdivision of time but, it is a minimal expression of a polyrhythm. We will call it **X against Y**.

X against Y

The right hand is subdividing the beat or measure by X (or playing X amount of notes per beat or measure) while the left hand is doing it with Y amount of notes.

Ex. RH in quarter notes, LH in eighth notes. That's **"1 against 2"**.

A true polyrhythm would be: RH plays eighth triplets, LH plays eighth notes or **"3 against 2"**.

The piano player must be able to perform all these subdivisions and polyrhythms since they are the foundation of all polyphonic music. For example: we must be able to shift from **2 against 1** into **1 against 2** (like in baroque music) without any problems, or to play **3 against 4** keeping a steady tempo and evenly distributing the subdivisions with no accents or gaps in the lines.

The exercises in this book are organized in 3 different kinds:
• *Preparing X against Y*
• *Playing X against Y*
• *Applying X against Y in a song*

Some of the simple X against Y, like 2 against 1, only have a playing mode version exercise, while others like the 3 against 4 have an extensive set of preparation exercises before you actually get into playing the polyrhythm.

Playing Polyrhythms is about expanding your aural perception and being able to perceive 2 different subdivisions of time at the same moment.

Concentrate on the main beat and shift your attention from one subdivision to the other.

Finger Repetitions 101

Place your hands in **C position.**

mDecks ID:

PTBv1-FR101

5 min.

Combination :

One finger at a time, same finger numbers in both hands.
LH-RH: 1-1 2-2 3-3 4-4 5-5

Repeat each finger combination 8 times. Metronome at 50.

This exercise is meant to be played slowly. Try to target each finger combination with a clean attack getting a good synchronized and balanced sound between both hands.

Relaxed shoulders and wrists.
Optimize finger movements with an articulate attack. Do not hit the keys to produce the sound, "push" the key.

Finger 4 is hard to control and also weak. Don't force it.

Previous Exercise

PTBv1-FR101

10

Listen to the sounds. Look for a round fat 2-note chord. If the attack in both notes is synchronized you will hear it.

Meditate while playing this exercise. Once you know it you can close your eyes and just listen. Let your brain develop any structures needed to play this exercise. Don't push for results.

"Without music, life would be a mistake." **Friedrich Wilhelm Nietzsche**

mDecks

MP3 download code
Q289L466

Ex. Page Reference
HB-2

Finger Repetitions 101

One Note. Same finger numbers. C Position. C Major.

Notes/Comments

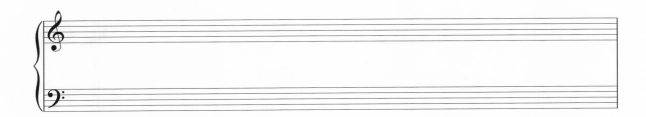

Finger Repetitions 102

Place your hands in **C position.**

mDecks ID:

PTBv1-FR102

5 min.

Previous Exercise

PTBv1-FR101

10

Combination :

One finger at a time, same note names in both hands.
LH-RH: 5-1 4-2 3-3 2-4 1-5

Repeat each finger combination 8 times. Metronome at 50.

This exercise is meant to be played slowly. Try to target each finger combination with a clean attack getting a good synchronized and balanced sound between both hands.

In this exercise you're playing in octaves, look for a fat sounding doubling - note.

Relaxed shoulders and wrists.
Optimize finger movements with an articulate attack. Do not hit the keys to produce the sound, "push" the key.

Finger 4 is combined with finger 2 helping focus (since finger 2 is an easy finger)

Meditate while playing this exercise. Once you know it you can close your eyes and just listen. Let your brain develop any structures needed to play this exercise. Don't push for results.

"Don't believe everything I tell you, but try my methods. If they help you, adopt them; if not, forget about them and find others." **Ehgon Petri**

MP3 download code

Q656L537

Ex. Page Reference

HB-2

Finger Repetitions 102

One Note. Same Note Names. C Position. C Major.

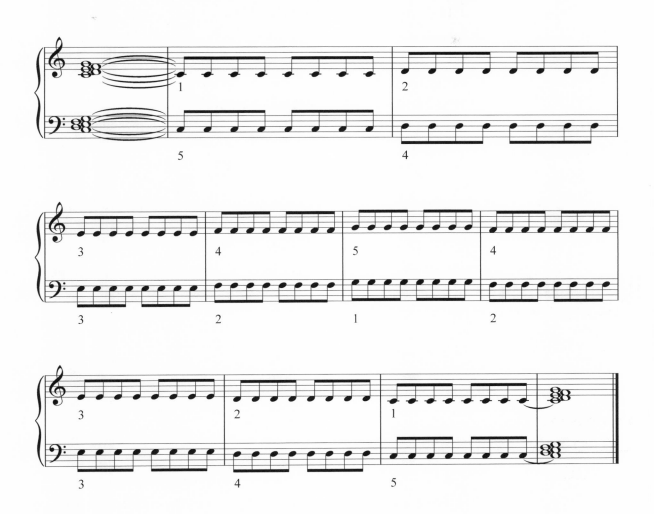

Notes/Comments

Finger Repetitions 201

Place your hands in **C position.**

mDecks ID:

PTBv1-FR201

7 min.

Combination :

Two fingers at a time, same finger numbers in both hands.
LH-RH: 12-12 13-13 14-14 15-15
LH-RH: 23-23 24-24 25-25
LH-RH: 34-34 35-35 45-45

Repeat each finger combination 8 times. Metronome at 50.

This exercise is meant to be played slowly. Try to target each finger combination with a clean attack getting a good synchronized and balanced sound between fingers and hands.

Relaxed shoulders and wrists.
Optimize finger movements with an articulate attack. Do not hit the keys to produce the sound, "push" the key.

Previous Exercise

PTBv1-FR101

10

You are using 4 fingers simultaneously. Listen and look for a perfect block-chord. Play all 4 notes together.

Meditate while playing this exercise. Once you know it you can close your eyes and just listen. Let your brain develop any structures needed to play this exercise. Don't push for results.

mDecks

MP3 download code

Q687L262

Ex. Page Reference

HB-2

Finger Repetitions 201

Two Notes. Same Finger Numbers. C Position. C Major.

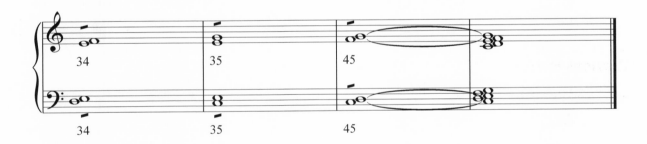

Notes/Comments

Finger Repetitions 202

Place your hands in **C position.**

mDecks ID:

PTBv1-FR202

7 min.

Combination :

Two fingers at a time, same note names in both hands.
LH-RH: 54-12 53-13 52-14 51-15
LH-RH: 43-23 42-24 41-25
LH-RH: 32-34 31-35 21-45

Repeat each finger combination 8 times. Metronome at 50.

This exercise is meant to be played slowly. Try to target each finger combination with a clean attack getting a good synchronized and balanced sound between fingers and hands.

Relaxed shoulders and wrists.
Optimize finger movements with an articulate attack. Do not hit the keys to produce the sound, "push" the key.

Previous Exercise

PTBv1-FR102

12

You are using 4 fingers simultaneously. Listen and look for a perfect block-chord. Play all 4 notes together.

In this exercise you're playing in octaves, look for a fat sounding doubling - 2 note cluster (chord).

Meditate while playing this exercise. Once you know it you can close your eyes and just listen. Let your brain develop any structures needed to play this exercise. Don't push for results.

"To play without passion is inexcusable!" **Ludwig van Beethoven**

mDecks

MP3 download code

Q615L672

Ex. Page Reference

HB-2

Finger Repetitions 202

Two Notes.Same Note Names. C Position. C Major.

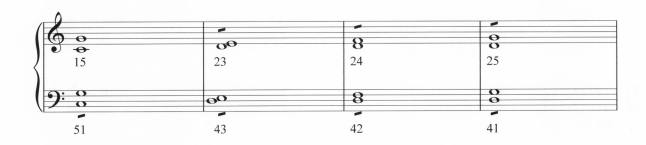

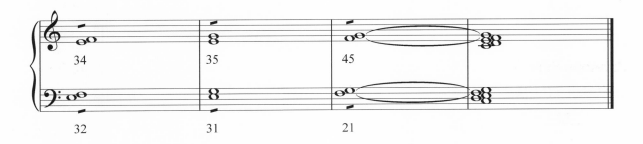

Notes/Comments

Finger Repetitions 301

Place your hands in **C position.**

mDecks ID:

PTBv1-FR301

7 min.

Combination :

Three fingers at a time, same finger numbers in both hands.
LH-RH: 123-123 124-124 125-125
LH-RH: 134-134 135-135 145-145
LH-RH: 234-234 235-235 245-245 345-345

Repeat each finger combination 8 times. Metronome at 50.

This exercise is meant to be played slowly. Try to target each finger combination with a clean attack getting a good synchronized and balanced sound between fingers and hands.

Relaxed shoulders and wrists.
Optimize finger movements with an articulate attack. Do not hit the keys to produce the sound, "push" the key.

Previous Exercise

PTBv1-FR201

14

You are using 6 fingers simultaneously. Listen and look for a perfect block-chord. Play all 6 notes together.

Playing 3 fingers simultaneously is almost the same as playing the 2 complementary fingers. You can concentrate on the fingers you are not playing and it would be like doing the Finger Repetition 201.

Meditate while playing this exercise. Once you know it you can close your eyes and just listen. Let your brain develop any structures needed to play this exercise. Don't push for results.

"Without craftsmanship, inspiration is a mere reed shaken in the wind." **Johannes Brahms**

mDecks

MP3 download code

Q624L161

Ex. Page Reference

HB-2

Finger Repetitions 301

Three Notes.Same Finger Numbers. C Position. C Major.

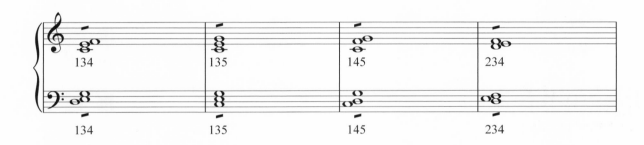

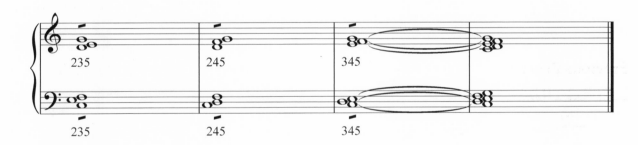

Notes/Comments

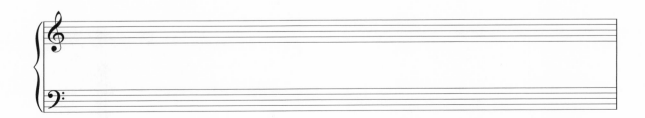

Finger Repetitions 302

Place your hands in **C position.**

mDecks ID:

PTBv1-FR302

7 min.

Combination :

Three fingers at a time, same note names in both hands.
LH-RH: 123-345 124-245 125-145
LH-RH: 134-235 135-135 145-125
LH-RH: 234-234 235-134 245-124 345-123

Repeat each finger combination 8 times. Metronome at 50.

This exercise is meant to be played slowly. Try to target each finger combination with a clean attack getting a good synchronized and balanced sound between fingers and hands.

Relaxed shoulders and wrists.
Optimize finger movements with an articulate attack. Do not hit the keys to produce the sound, "push" the key.

Previous Exercise

PTBv1-FR202

16

You are using 6 fingers simultaneously. Listen and look for a perfect block-chord. Play all 6 notes together. In this exercise you're playing in octaves, look for a fat sounding **doubling** - 3 note cluster (chord).

Playing 3 fingers simultaneously is almost the same as playing the 2 complementary fingers. You can concentrate on the fingers you are not playing and it would be like doing the Finger Repetition 202.

"Simplicity is the final achievement. After one has played a vast quantity of notes and more notes, it is simplicity that emerges as the crowning reward of art." **Frederic Chopin**

MP3 download code

 **Q825L030**

Ex. Page Reference

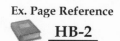 **HB-2**

Finger Repetitions 302

Three Notes.Same Note Names. C Position. C Major.

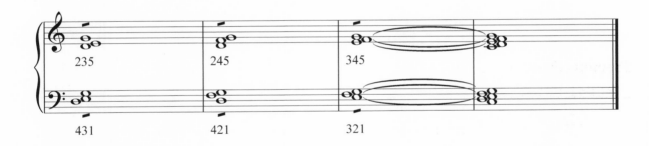

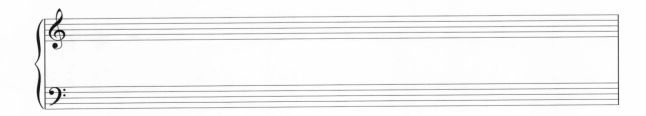

Notes/Comments

Finger Repetitions 401

Place your hands in **C position.**

mDecks ID:

PTBv1-FR401

5 min.

Combination :

Four fingers at a time, same finger numbers in both hands.
LH-RH: 1234-1234, 1235-1235, 1245-1245, 1345-1345, 2345-2345

Repeat each finger combination 8 times. Metronome at 50.

This exercise is meant to be played slowly. Try to target each finger combination with a clean attack getting a good synchronized and balanced sound between fingers and hands.

Relaxed shoulders and wrists.
Optimize finger movements with an articulate attack. Do not hit the keys to produce the sound, "push" the key.

You are using 8 fingers simultaneously. Listen and look for a perfect block-chord. Play all 8 notes together.

Previous Exercise

PTBv1-FR101

10

Playing 4 fingers simultaneously is almost the same as playing the 1 complementary finger. You can concentrate on the finger you are not playing and it would be like doing the Finger Repetition 101.

Meditate while playing this exercise. Once you know it you can close your eyes and just listen. Let your brain develop any structures needed to play this exercise. Don't push for results.

"If a composer could say what he had to say in words he would not bother trying to say it in music." **Gustav Mahler**

mDecks

MP3 download code
Q444L526

Ex. Page Reference
HB-2

Finger Repetitions 401

Four Notes.Same Finger Numbers. C Position. C Major.

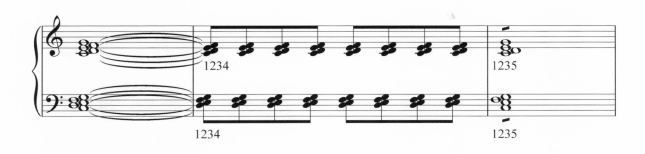

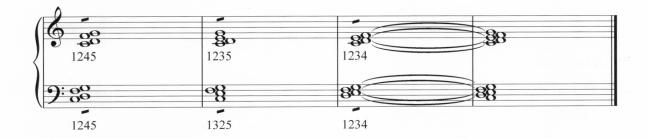

Notes/Comments

Finger Repetitions 402

Place your hands in **C position.**

mDecks ID:
PTBv1-FR402

5 min.

Combination :

Four fingers at a time, same note names in both hands.
LH-RH: 1234-2345, 1235-1345, 1245-1245, 1345-1235, 2345-1234

Repeat each finger combination 8 times. Metronome at 50.

This exercise is meant to be played slowly. Try to target each finger combination with a clean attack getting a good synchronized and balanced sound between fingers and hands.

Relaxed shoulders and wrists.
Optimize finger movements with an articulate attack. Do not hit the keys to produce the sound, "push" the key.

Previous Exercise
PTBv1-FR102

12

You are using 8 fingers simultaneously. Listen and look for a perfect block-chord. Play all 8 notes together. In this exercise you're playing in octaves, look for a fat sounding **doubling** - 4 note cluster (chord).

Playing 4 fingers simultaneously is almost the same as playing the 1 complementary finger. You can concentrate on the finger you are not playing and it would be like doing the Finger Repetition 102.

Meditate while playing this exercise. Once you know it you can close your eyes and just listen. Let your brain develop any structures needed to play this exercise. Don't push for results.

"I sit down to the piano regularly at nine-o'clock in the morning and Mesdames les Muses have learned to be on time for that rendezvous." **Pyotr Ilich Tchaikovsky**

MP3 download code
Q911L923

Ex. Page Reference
HB-2

Finger Repetitions 402

Four Notes.Same Note Names. C Position. C Major.

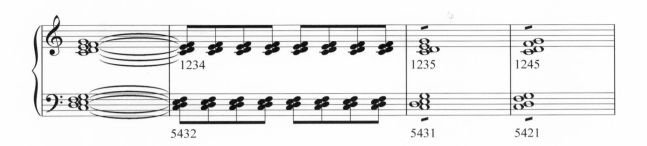

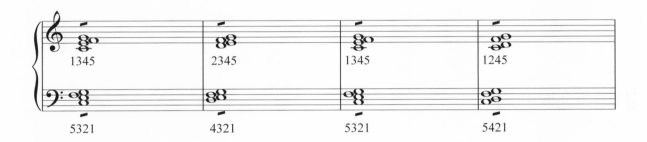

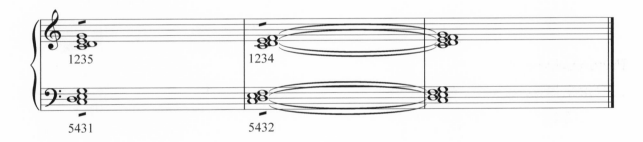

Notes/Comments

Finger Repetitions 111

Place your hands in **F#7 Chord position.**

(as shown in keyboard diagram)

mDecks ID:

PTBv1-FR111

5 min.

Combination :

One finger at a time, same finger numbers in both hands.
LH-RH: 1-1 2-2 3-3 4-4 5-5

Repeat each finger combination 8 times. Metronome at 50.

This exercise is meant to be played slowly. Try to target each finger combination with a clean attack getting a good synchronized and balanced sound between both hands. This F#7 position is for bigger hands an it will stretch muscles and tendons.

Relaxed shoulders and wrists.
Optimize finger movements with an articulate attack. Do not hit the keys to produce the sound, "push" the key.

Previous Exercise

PTBv1-FR101

10

Finger 4 is hard to control and also weak. Don't force it.
When playing black keys the hand should adjust shifting slightly to the inside of the keyboard (closer to the fall-board)

Listen to the sounds. Look for a round fat 2-note chord. If the attack in both notes is synchronized you will hear it.

Meditate while playing this exercise. Once you know it you can close your eyes and just listen. Let your brain develop any structures needed to play this exercise. Don't push for results.

"I was meant to be a composer and will be I'm sure. Don't ask me to try to forget this unpleasant thing and go play football - please." **Samuel Barber**

mDecks

MP3 download code

Q797L201

Ex. Page Reference

HB-2

Finger Repetitions 111

One Note. Same finger numbers. F#7 Chord. B Major.

Notes/Comments

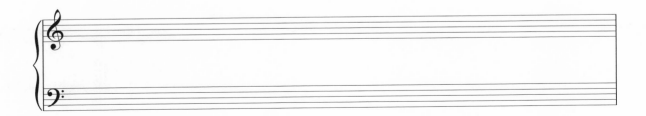

Finger Repetitions 112

Place your hands in **F#7 Chord position.**
(as shown in keyboard diagram)

mDecks ID:

PTBv1-FR112

Combination :

One finger at a time, same note names in both hands.
LH-RH: 5-1 4-2 3-3 2-4 1-5

5 min.

Repeat each finger combination 8 times. Metronome at 50.

This exercise is meant to be played slowly. Try to target each finger combination with a clean attack getting a good synchronized and balanced sound between both hands. This F#7 position is for bigger hands an it will stretch muscles and tendons.

In this exercise you're playing in octaves, look for a fat sounding doubling - note.

Relaxed shoulders and wrists.

Previous Exercise

PTBv1-FR102

12

Optimize finger movements with an articulate attack. Do not hit the keys to produce the sound, "push" the key.

Finger 4 is combined with finger 2 helping focus (since finger 2 is an easy finger)

Meditate while playing this exercise. Once you know it you can close your eyes and just listen. Let your brain develop any structures needed to play this exercise. Don't push for results.

"Art is the triumph over chaos." **John Cheever**

mDecks

MP3 download code

Q198L965

Ex. Page Reference

HB-2

mDecks.com   28

Finger Repetitions 112

One Note. Same Note Names. F#7 Chord. B Major.

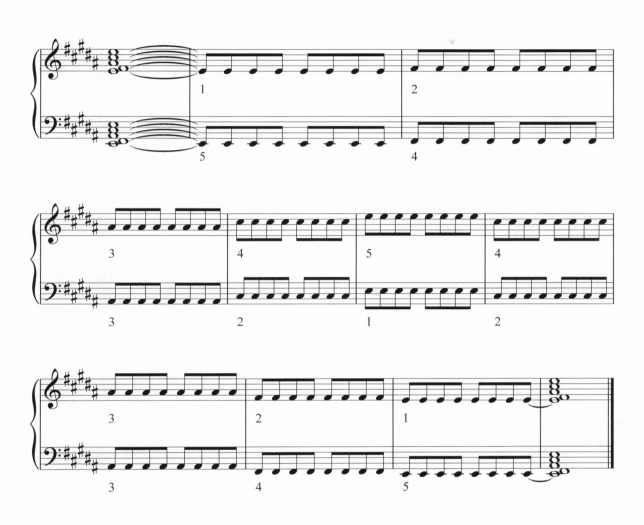

Notes/Comments

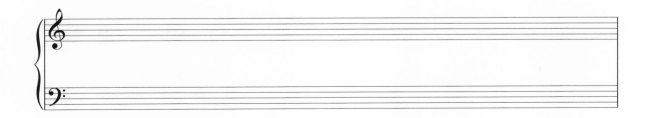

Finger Repetitions 211

Place your hands in **F#7 Chord position.**
(as shown in keyboard diagram)

mDecks ID:

PTBv1-FR211

7 min.

Combination :

Two fingers at a time, same finger numbers in both hands.
LH-RH: 12-12 13-13 14-14 15-15
LH-RH: 23-23 24-24 25-25
LH-RH: 34-34 35-35 45-45

Repeat each finger combination 8 times. Metronome at 50.

This exercise is meant to be played slowly. Try to target each finger combination with a clean attack getting a good synchronized and balanced sound between fingers and hands. This F#7 position is for bigger hands an it will stretch muscles and tendons.

Relaxed shoulders and wrists.
Optimize finger movements with an articulate attack. Do not hit the keys to produce the sound, "push" the key.

Previous Exercise

PTBv1-FR201

14

You are using 4 fingers simultaneously. Listen and look for a perfect block-chord. Play all 4 notes together.

Meditate while playing this exercise. Once you know it you can close your eyes and just listen. Let your brain develop any structures needed to play this exercise. Don't push for results.

"Play the music, not the instrument. " **Author Unknown**

MP3 download code

Q495L992

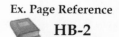

Ex. Page Reference

HB-2

Finger Repetitions 211

Two Notes.Same Finger Numbers. F#7 Chord. B Major.

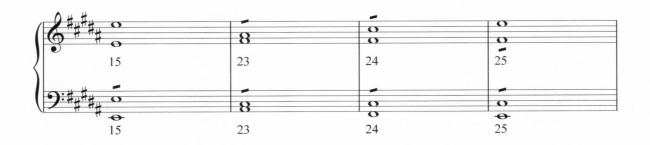

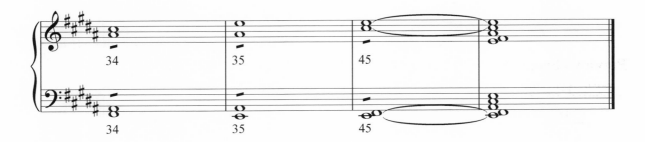

Notes/Comments

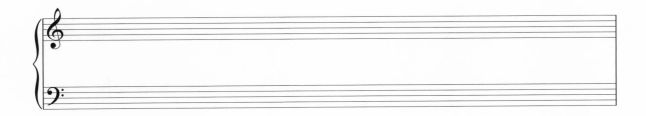

Finger Repetitions 212

Place your hands in **F#7 Chord position.**
(as shown in keyboard diagram)

mDecks ID:
PTBv1-FR212

7 min.

Previous Exercise
PTBv1-FR202

16

Combination :

Two fingers at a time, same note names in both hands.
LH-RH: 54-12 53-13 52-14 51-15
LH-RH: 43-23 42-24 41-25
LH-RH: 32-34 31-35 21-45

Repeat each finger combination 8 times. Metronome at 50.

This exercise is meant to be played slowly. Try to target each finger combination with a clean attack getting a good synchronized and balanced sound between fingers and hands. This F#7 position is for bigger hands an it will stretch muscles and tendons.

Relaxed shoulders and wrists.
Optimize finger movements with an articulate attack. Do not hit the keys to produce the sound, "push" the key.

You are using 4 fingers simultaneously. Listen and look for a perfect block-chord. Play all 4 notes together.

In this exercise you're playing in octaves, look for a fat sounding doubling - 2 note chord.

Meditate while playing this exercise. Once you know it you can close your eyes and just listen. Let your brain develop any structures needed to play this exercise. Don't push for results.

"The pause is as important as the note. " **Truman Fisher**

MP3 download code

Q390L079

Ex. Page Reference
HB-2

Finger Repetitions 212
Two Notes.Same Note Names. F#7 Chord. B Major.

Notes/Comments

Finger Repetitions 311

Place your hands in **F#7 Chord position.**

(as shown in keyboard diagram)

mDecks ID:

PTBv1-FR311

7 min.

Combination :

Three fingers at a time, same finger numbers in both hands.

LH-RH: 123-123 124-124 125-125

LH-RH: 134-134 135-135 145-145

LH-RH: 234-234 235=235 245-245 345-345

Repeat each finger combination 8 times. Metronome at 50.

This exercise is meant to be played slowly. Try to target each finger combination with a clean attack getting a good synchronized and balanced sound between fingers and hands. This F#7 position is for bigger hands an it will stretch muscles and tendons.

Relaxed shoulders and wrists.

Optimize finger movements with an articulate attack. Do not hit the keys to produce the sound, "push" the key.

Previous Exercise

PTBv1-FR301

18

You are using 6 fingers simultaneously. Listen and look for a perfect block-chord. Play all 6 notes together.

Playing 3 fingers simultaneously is almost the same as playing the 2 complementary fingers. You can concentrate on the fingers you are not playing and it would be like doing the Finger Repetition 201.

"Too many pieces of music finish too long after the end." **Igor Stravinsky**

mDecks

MP3 download code

Q022L866

Ex. Page Reference

HB-2

mDecks.com

34

Finger Repetitions 311

Three Notes.Same Finger Numbers. F#7 Chord. B Major.

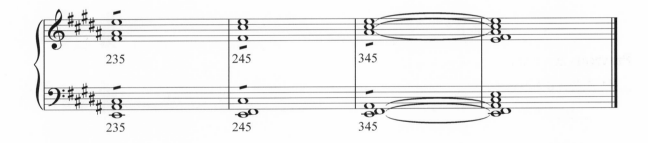

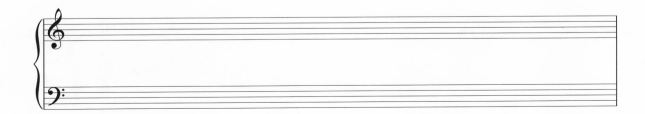

Notes/Comments

Finger Repetitions 312

Place your hands in **F#7 Chord position.**
(as shown in keyboard diagram)

mDecks ID:

PTBv1-FR312

7 min.

Previous Exercise

PTBv1-FR302

20

Combination :
Three fingers at a time, same note names in both hands.
LH-RH: 123-345 124-245 125-145
LH-RH: 134-235 135-135 145-125
LH-RH: 234-234 235=134 245-124 345-123

Repeat each finger combination 8 times. Metronome at 50.

This exercise is meant to be played slowly. Try to target each finger combination with a clean attack getting a good synchronized and balanced sound between fingers and hands. This F#7 position is for bigger hands an it will stretch muscles and tendons.

Relaxed shoulders and wrists.
Optimize finger movements with an articulate attack. Do not hit the keys to produce the sound, "push" the key.

You are using 6 fingers simultaneously. Listen and look for a perfect block-chord. Play all 6 notes together. In this exercise you're playing in octaves, look for a fat sounding **doubling** - 3 note chord.

Playing 3 fingers simultaneously is almost the same as playing the 2 complementary fingers.

"Music is moonlight in the gloomy night of life. " **Jean Paul Richter**

MP3 download code
Q298L088

Ex. Page Reference
HB-2

Finger Repetitions 312

Three Notes.Same Note Names. F#7 Chord. B Major.

Notes/Comments

Fingers Control, Independence, Balance & Strength
Rhythmic Subdivisions and Essential Polyrhythms

Finger Repetitions 411

Place your hands in **F#7 Chord position.**
(as shown in keyboard diagram)

mDecks ID:
PTBv1-FR411

5 min.

Combination :
Three fingers at a time, same note names in both hands.
LH-RH: 5432-1234,5431-1235, 5421-1245, 3521-1345, 4321-2345

Repeat each finger combination 8 times. Metronome at 50.
This exercise is meant to be played slowly. Try to target each finger combination with a clean attack getting a good synchronized and balanced sound between fingers and hands. This F#7 position is for bigger hands an it will stretch muscles and tendons.

Relaxed shoulders and wrists.
Optimize finger movements with an articulate attack. Do not hit the keys to produce the sound, "push" the key.

You are using 8 fingers simultaneously. Listen and look for a perfect block-chord. Play all 8 notes together.

Playing 4 fingers simultaneously is almost the same as playing the 1 complementary finger. You can concentrate on the finger you are not playing and it would be like doing the Finger Repetition 111.

Meditate while playing this exercise. Once you know it you can close your eyes and just listen. Let your brain develop any structures needed to play this exercise. Don't push for results.

Previous Exercise
PTBv1-FR401

22

"I have my own particular sorrows, loves, delights; and you have yours. But sorrow, gladness, yearning, hope, love, belong to all of us, in all times and in all places. Music is the only means whereby we feel these emotions in their universality. " **H.A. Overstreet**

mDecks

MP3 download code
Q256L264

Ex. Page Reference
HB-2

Finger Repetitions 411

Four Notes.Same Finger Numbers. F#7 Chord. B Major.

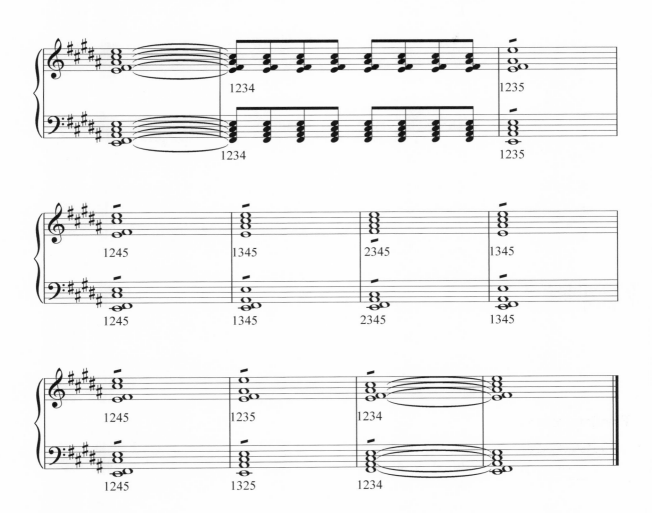

Notes/Comments

Finger Repetitions 412

Place your hands in **F#7 Chord position.**
(as shown in keyboard diagram)

mDecks ID:

PTBv1-FR412

5 min.

Combination :

Three fingers at a time, same note names in both hands.
LH-RH: 1234-2345, 1235-1345, 1245-1245, 1345-1235, 2345-1234

Repeat each finger combination 8 times. Metronome at 50.

This exercise is meant to be played slowly. Try to target each finger combination with a clean attack getting a good synchronized and balanced sound between fingers and hands. This F#7 position is for bigger hands an it will stretch muscles and tendons.

Relaxed shoulders and wrists.
Optimize finger movements with an articulate attack. Do not hit the keys to produce the sound, "push" the key.

Previous Exercise

PTBv1-FR402

24

You are using 8 fingers simultaneously. Listen and look for a perfect block-chord. Play all 8 notes together. In this exercise you're playing in octaves, look for a fat sounding **doubling** - 4 note chord.

Playing 4 fingers simultaneously is almost the same as playing the 1 complementary finger. You can concentrate on the finger you are not playing and it would be like doing the Finger Repetition 111.

"In music the passions enjoy themselves. " **Nietzsche**

MP3 download code

Q191L665

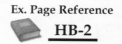
Ex. Page Reference

HB-2

Finger Repetitions 412

Four Notes. Same Note Names. F#7 Chord. B Major.

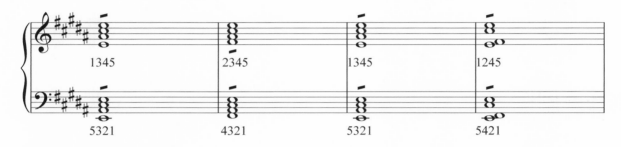

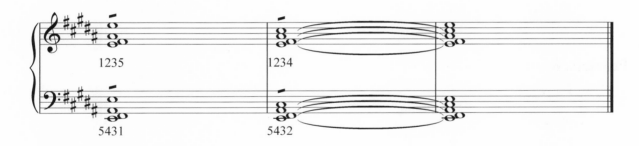

Notes/Comments

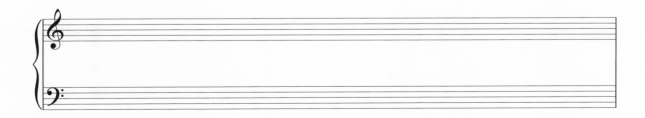

Finger Repetitions C21

Place your hands in Bb Pentatonic - F Inversion.
(look at keyboard diagram)

mDecks ID:
PTBv1-FRC21

10 min.

Complementary Fingers Combination :
One finger and the complementary 4 **fingers** on the other hand.
LH-RH: 1-2345, 2-1345, 3-1245, 4-1235, 5-1234
LH-RH: 2345-1, 1345-2, 1245-3, 1235-4, 1234-5

Repeat each finger combination 8 times. Metronome at 50.

This exercise is meant to be played slowly. Try to target each finger combination with a clean attack getting a good synchronized and balanced sound between fingers and hands.

This is a **challenging** combination. Always focus on the hand that is playing the least amount of notes first and add the fingers you are not playing on the other hand.

Previous Exercise
PTBv1-FR411

38

Relaxed shoulders and wrists.
Optimize finger movements with an articulate attack. Do not hit the keys to produce the sound, "push" the key.

Meditate while playing this exercise. Once you know it you can close your eyes and just listen. Let your brain develop any structures needed to play this exercise. Don't push for results.

"It is a mistake to think that the practice of my art has become easy to me. I assure you, dear friend, no one has given so much care to the study of composition as I. There is scarcely a famous master in music whose works I have not frequently and diligently studied." **Wolfgang Amadeus Mozart**

mDecks

MP3 download code
Q520L821

Ex. Page Reference
HB-2

Finger Repetitions C21

Complementary Fingers 1 vs.4. Bb Pentatonic. F Inversion..

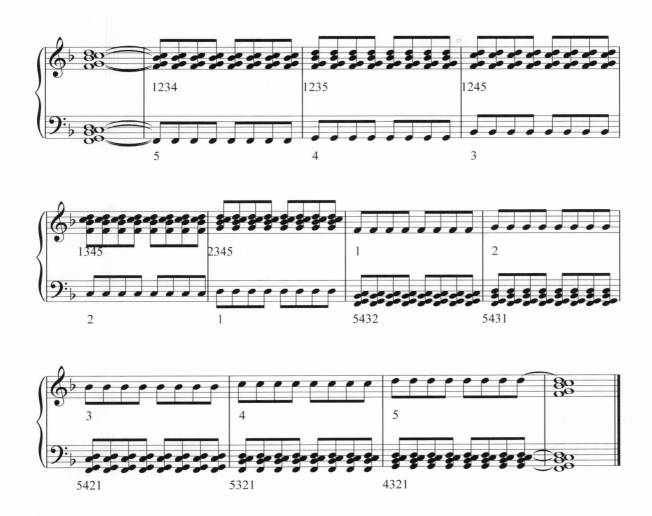

Notes/Comments

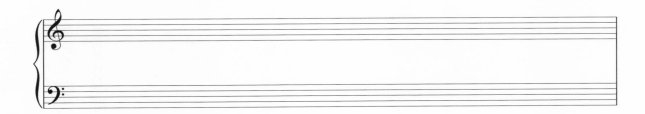

Finger Repetitions C22

Place your hands in Bb Pentatonic - F Inversion.
(look at keyboard diagram)

mDecks ID:

PTBv1-FRC22

10 min.

Complementary Notes Combination :

One finger and the complementary 4 **notes** on the other hand.
LH-RH: 1-1234, 2-1235, 3-1245, 4-1345, 5-2345
LH-RH: 1234-1, 1235-2, 1245-3, 1345-4, 2345-5

Repeat each finger combination 8 times. Metronome at 50.

This exercise is meant to be played slowly. Try to target each finger combination with a clean attack getting a good synchronized and balanced sound between fingers and hands.

This is a challenging combination. Always focus on the hand that is playing the least amount of notes first and add the fingers you are not playing on the other hand.

Previous Exercise

PTBv1-FR412

40

Each combination spell the same Bb Pentatonic 5-note chord in different voicings. Listen for the complete chord sound.

Relaxed shoulders and wrists.
Optimize finger movements with an articulate attack. Do not hit the keys to produce the sound, "push" the key.

Meditate while playing this exercise. Once you know it you can close your eyes and just listen. Let your brain develop any structures needed to play this exercise. Don't push for results.

"If a composer could say what he had to say in words he would not bother trying to say it in music. " **Gustav Mahler**

MP3 download code

Q174L527

Ex. Page Reference

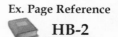

HB-2

Finger Repetitions C22

Complementary Notes 1vs.4. Bb Pentatonic. F Inversion..

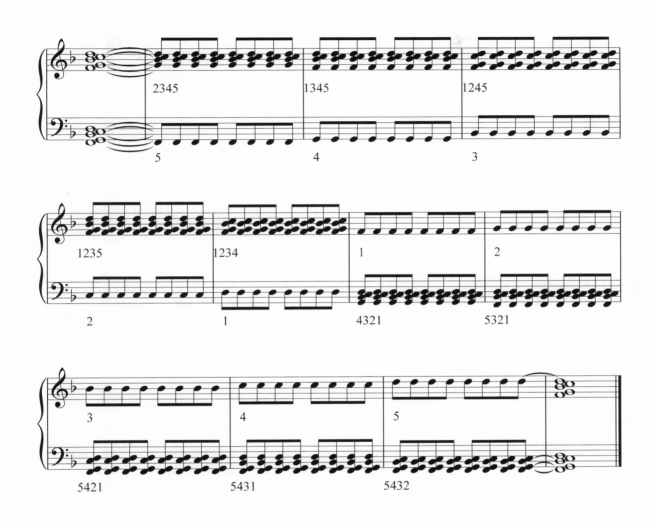

Notes/Comments

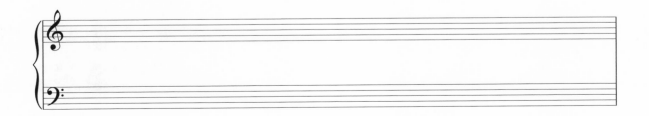

Finger Repetitions C23

Place your hands in Bb Pentatonic - F Inversion.
(look at keyboard diagram)

mDecks ID:

PTBv1-FRC23

10 min.

Complementary Fingers Combination :

Two fingers plus the complementary 3 **fingers** on the other hand.
LH-RH: 12-345, 13-245, 14-235, 15-234, 23-145, 24-135, 25-134,
34-125, 35-124, 45-123
LH-RH: 345-12, 245-13, 235-14, 234-15, 145-23, 135-24, 134-25,
125-34, 124-35, 123-45

Repeat each finger combination 8 times. Metronome at 50.

*This exercise is meant to be played slowly. Try to target each finger
combination with a clean attack getting a good synchronized and
balanced sound between fingers and hands.*

This is a challenging combination. Always focus on the hand that
is playing the least amount of notes first and add the fingers you
are not playing on the other hand.

Previous Exercise

PTBv1-FR411

38

Relaxed shoulders and wrists.
*Optimize finger movements with an articulate attack. Do not hit the
keys to produce the sound, "push" the key.*

*Meditate while playing this exercise. Once you know it you can close
your eyes and just listen. Let your brain develop any structures needed
to play this exercise. Don't push for results.*

"The wise musicians are those who play what they can master" **Duke Ellington**

MP3 download code

Q391L553

Ex. Page Reference

HB-2

Finger Repetitions C23
Complementary Fingers 2 vs.3. Bb Pentatonic. F Inversion..

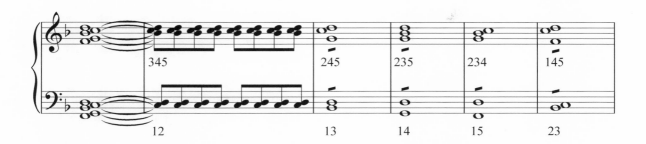

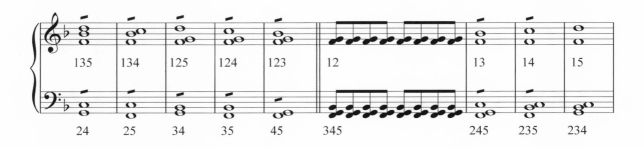

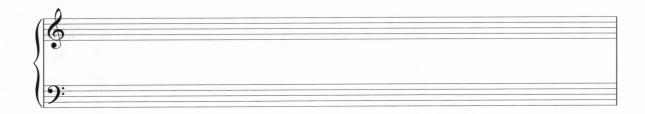

Notes/Comments

Finger Repetitions C24

Place your hands in Bb Pentatonic - F Inversion.
(look at keyboard diagram)

mDecks ID:

PTBv1-FRC24

10 min.

Complementary Notes Combination :

Two fingers and the complementary 3 **notes** on the other hand.
LH-RH: 12-123, 13-124, 14-134, 15-234, 23-125, 24-135, 25-235, 34
-145, 35-245, 45-345
LH-RH: 123-12, 124-13, 134-14, 234-15, 125-23, 135-24, 235-25, 145
-34, 245-35, 345-45

Repeat each finger combination 8 times. Metronome at 50.
*This exercise is meant to be played slowly. Try to target each finger
combination with a clean attack getting a good synchronized and
balanced sound between fingers and hands.*

This is a challenging combination. Always focus on the hand that
is playing the least amount of notes first and add the fingers you
are not playing on the other hand.

Previous Exercise
PTBv1-FR412
40

Each combination spell the same Bb Pentatonic 5-note chord in
different voicings. Listen for the complete chord sound.

*Relaxed shoulders and wrists.
Optimize finger movements with an articulate attack. Do not hit the
keys to produce the sound, "push" the key.*

*Meditate while playing this exercise. Once you know it you can close
your eyes and just listen. Let your brain develop any structures needed
to play this exercise. Don't push for results.*

"After silence, that which comes nearest to expressing the inexpressible is music." **Aldous Huxley**

MP3 download code

Q008L889

Ex. Page Reference

HB-2

Finger Repetitions C24

Complementary Notes 2 vs.3. Bb Pentatonic. F Inversion..

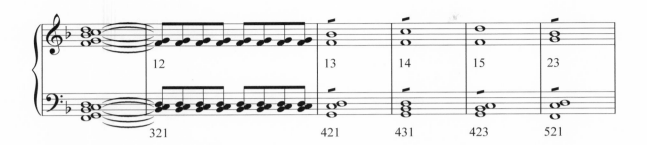

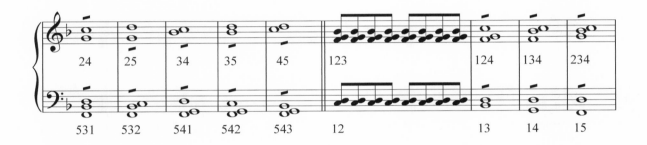

Notes/Comments

X Against Y 1a2

Place your hands in C Position

mDecks ID:

PTBv1-XY1a2

5 min.

Playing 2 Notes against 1 Note :

This is simple pattern of eighth notes in one hand against a repeated note in the other hand.

Should be played at all tempos. Metronome from 50 to 200 per quarter note.

Notes that attack at the same time in both hands should be perfectly synchronized between each other and with the metronome.

You can first try playing with an accent on downbeats. Then play it without accents.

Avoid playing staccato. Try to **focus** your **movements** on your **fingers** and **not** on your **wrists.**

Previous Exercise

PTBv1-XY1a2

50

Left hand is accustomed to playing the longer notes. Don't feel disappointed when the tempos become to fast for your left hand to follow since this is very normal.

Meditate while playing this exercise. Once you know it you can close your eyes and just listen. Let your brain develop any structures needed to play this exercise. Don't push for results.

"If in the after life there is not music, we will have to import it. " **Doménico Cieri Estrada**

mDecks

MP3 download code

Q236L597

Ex. Page Reference

HB-3

X Against Y 1a2
C Position. Simple Pattern

Notes/Comments

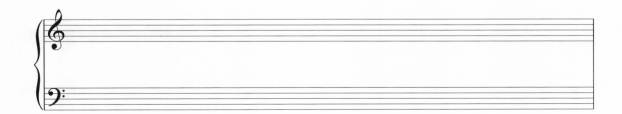

X Against Y 1a3

Place your hands in C Position

Playing 3 Notes against 1 Note :

This is simple pattern of eighth notes triplets in one hand against a repeated note in the other hand.

mDecks ID:

PTBv1-XY1a3

5 min.

Should be played at all tempos. Metronome from 50 to 160 per quarter note.

Notes that attack at the same time in both hands should be perfectly synchronized between each other and with the metronome.

You can first try playing with an accent on downbeats. Then play it without accents.

Avoid playing staccato. Try to **focus** your **movements** on your **fingers** and **not** on your **wrists.**

Previous Exercise

PTBv1-XY1a2

50

Left hand is accustomed to playing the longer notes. Don't feel disappointed when the tempos become to fast for your left hand to follow since this is very normal.

Meditate while playing this exercise. Once you know it you can close your eyes and just listen. Let your brain develop any structures needed to play this exercise. Don't push for results.

"Lesser artists borrow, great artists steal." **Igor Stravinsky**

MP3 download code

 Q489L043

Ex. Page Reference

HB-3

X Against Y 1a3

C Position. Simple Pattern

Notes/Comments

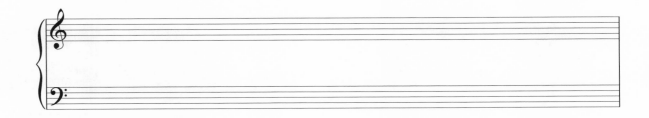

X Against Y 1a4

Place your hands in C Position

mDecks ID:

PTBv1-XY1a4

5 min.

Playing 4 Notes against 1 Note :

This is simple pattern of sixteenth notes in one hand against a repeated note scale in the other hand.

Should be played at all tempos. Metronome from 50 to 140 per quarter note.

Notes that attack at the same time in both hands should be perfectly synchronized between each other and with the metronome.

You can first try playing with an accent on downbeats. Then play it without accents.

Avoid playing staccato. Your wrists should smoothly follow the oscillating pattern of the sixteenth notes

Previous Exercise

PTBv1-XY1a2

50

Left hand is accustomed to playing the longer notes. Don't feel disappointed when the tempos become to fast for your left hand to follow since this is very normal.

Meditate while playing this exercise. Once you know it you can close your eyes and just listen. Let your brain develop any structures needed to play this exercise. Don't push for results.

"Music expresses feeling and thought, without language; it was below and before speech, and it is above and beyond all words. " **Robert G. Ingersoll**

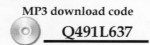

MP3 download code

Q491L637

Ex. Page Reference

HB-3

X Against Y 1a4

C Position. Simple Pattern

Notes/Comments

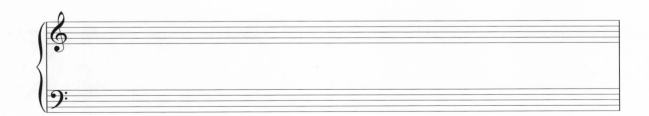

X Against Y 1b2

Place your hands in C Position

mDecks ID:

PTBv1-XY1b2

5 min.

Playing 2 Notes against 1 Note in alternating patterns:

This is a more complicated game of switching the 2 against 1 from one hand to the other.

Should be played at all tempos. Metronome from 50 to 180 per quarter note.

Notes that attack at the same time in both hands should be perfectly synchronized between each other and with the metronome.

Avoid playing staccato in non repeated notes. (Repeated notes can be played stacatto or portato).

The shifting from 2vs1 to 1vs2 is very important for the development of hand coordination and timing control, also very common in baroque music (such as J.S.Bach's music)

Previous Exercise

PTBv1-XY1a2

50

"For a long time I limited myself to one color—as a form of discipline." **Pablo Picasso**

mDecks

MP3 download code
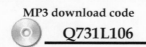
Q731L106

Ex. Page Reference

HB-3

mDecks.com

56

X Against Y 1b2

C Position. Alternations

Notes/Comments

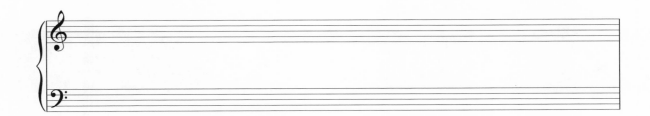

X Against Y 1b3

Place your hands in C Position

mDecks ID:

PTBv1-XY1b3

5 min.

Playing 3 Notes against 1 Note in alternating patterns:

This is a more complicated game of switching the 3 against 1 from one hand to the other.

Should be played at all tempos. Metronome from 50 to 140 per quarter note.

Notes that attack at the same time in both hands should be perfectly synchronized between each other and with the metronome.

Avoid playing staccato in non repeated notes. (Repeated notes can be played stacatto or portato).

The shifting from 2vs1 to 1vs2 is very important for the development of hand coordination and timing control, also very common in baroque music (such as J.S.Bach's music)

Previous Exercise

PTBv1-XY1a3

52

Concentrate in your left hand triplets, verifying they are played correctly, without skipping notes and in tempo.

mDecks

MP3 download code

Q304L377

Ex. Page Reference

HB-3

X Against Y 1b3

C Postition. Alternations

Notes/Comments

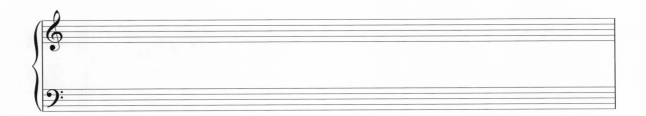

Finger Repetitions

X Against Y 1b4

Place your hands in C Position

mDecks ID:

PTBv1-XY1b4

5 min.

Playing 4 Notes against 1 Note in alternating patterns:

This is a more complicated game of switching the 4 against 1 from one hand to the other.

Should be played at all tempos. Metronome from 50 to 125 per quarter note.

Notes that attack at the same time in both hands should be perfectly synchronized between each other and with the metronome.

Avoid playing staccato in non repeated notes. (Repeated notes can be played stacatto or portato).

The shifting from 2vs1 to 1vs2 is very important for the development of hand coordination and timing control, also very common in baroque music (such as J.S.Bach's music)

Previous Exercise

PTBv1-XY1a4

54

Concentrate in your left hand sixteenths, verifying they are played correctly, without skipping notes and in tempo.

"Music is the shorthand of emotion. " **Leo Tolstoy**

MP3 download code

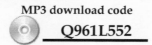

Q961L552

Ex. Page Reference

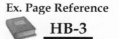

HB-3

X Against Y 1b4

C Position. Alternations

Notes/Comments

X Against Y 2a3

Place your hands in C Position

mDecks ID:

PTBv1-XY2a3

7 min.

Preparing 2 notes against 3 notes:

This is the first exercise for preparing playing the 2 against 3 polyrhythm.

Should be played at all tempos. Metronome from 50 to 200 per quarter note.

Playing Polyrhythms is about expanding your aural perception and being able to perceive 2 different subdivisions of time at the same moment.

Concentrate on the main beat and shift your attention from one subdivision to the other.

In this exercise the only subdivision is in the eighth notes on the 2nd beat of the measure.

Previous Exercise

PTBv1-XY1a3

52

This simple pattern is the base for playing 2 against 3. If you can play this you can play 2vs3!

"Why waste money on psychotherapy when you can listen to the B Minor Mass? " **Michael Torke**

mDecks

MP3 download code

Q133L845

Ex. Page Reference

HB-3

X Against Y 2a3

C Position. Preparing 2 against 3

Notes/Comments

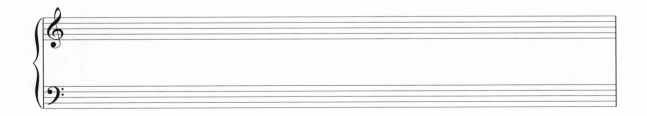

X Against Y 2b3

Place your hands in C Position to start but you will be shifting.

Preparing 2 notes against 3 notes:

This is the 2nd exercise for preparing playing the 2 against 3 polyrhythm.

Should be played at all tempos. Metronome from 50 to 140 per quarter note.

Playing Polyrhythms is about expanding your aural perception and being able to perceive 2 different subdivisions of time at the same moment.

Concentrate on the main beat and shift your attention from one subdivision to the other.

Only the first finger on each hand will be used. You'll be doing a drum approach to piano playing. In this exercise the only subdivision is in the eighth notes on the 2nd beat of the measure.

There's a 2 measure pattern. In the first measure of the pattern you are only playing with your **right hand**. The second measure is exactly the same but playing one note with your **left hand**. Try to make them sound exactly the same, even though you're playing them differently.

mDecks ID:

PTBv1-XY2b3

7 min.

Previous Exercise

PTBv1-XY2a3

62

"To listen is an effort, and just to hear is no merit. A duck hears also." **Igor Stravinsky**

X Against Y 2b3

Shifting Positions. Preparing 2 against 3

Notes/Comments

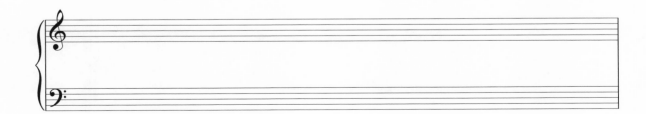

X Against Y 2c3

Place your hands in C Position.

Preparing 2 notes against 3 notes:

Play the independent note an 8ve apart.

mDecks ID:

PTBv1-XY2c3

7 min.

Should be played at all tempos. Metronome from 50 to 140 per quarter note.

Playing Polyrhythms is about expanding your aural perception and being able to perceive 2 different subdivisions of time at the same moment.

Concentrate on the main beat and shift your attention from one subdivision to the other.

In this exercise the only subdivision is in the eighth notes on the 2nd beat of the measure.

Previous Exercise

PTBv1-XY2b3

64

There's a 2 measure pattern. In the first measure of the pattern you are only playing with your **left hand**. The second measure is exactly the same but playing one note with your **right hand**. Try to make them sound rhythmically the same, even though they are different.

A difference with exercise **XY3b2**, this exercise has the **right-hand** note being played an 8ve apart, which makes it stand out from the pattern. **Pay close attention to where this note lands in the pattern.**

"Music is what feelings sound like. " **Author Unknown**

mDecks

MP3 download code

Q251L552

Ex. Page Reference

HB-3

X Against Y 2c3

C Position. Preparing 2 against 3

Notes/Comments

X Against Y 3b2

Place your hands in C Position to start but you will be shifting.

Preparing 3 notes against 2 notes:

Same as **XY2b3** but with the solo note in the **right hand.**

mDecks ID:

PTBv1-XY3b2

7 min.

Should be played at all tempos. Metronome from 50 to 140 per quarter note.

Playing Polyrhythms is about expanding your aural perception and being able to perceive 2 different subdivisions of time at the same moment.

Concentrate on the main beat and shift your attention from one subdivision to the other.

Only the first finger on each hand will be used. You'll be doing a drum approach to piano playing. In this exercise the only subdivision is in the eighth notes on the 2nd beat of the measure.

Previous Exercise

PTBv1-XY2b3

64

There's a 2 measure pattern. In the first measure of the pattern you are only playing with your **left hand**. The second measure is exactly the same but playing one note with your **right hand**. Try to make them sound exactly the same, even though you're playing them differently.

"Technical skill is mastery of complexity, while creativity is mastery of simplicity" **Erik Christopher Zeeman**

MP3 download code

Q405L817

Ex. Page Reference

HB-3

mDecks

X Against Y 3b2

Shifting Positions. Preparing 3 against 2

Notes/Comments

X Against Y 3c2

Place your hands in C Position.

Preparing 2 notes against 3 notes:

Same as **XY2c3** but with the solo note in the **right hand.**

mDecks ID:

PTBv1-XY3c2

7 min.

Should be played at all tempos. Metronome from 50 to 140 per quarter note.

Playing Polyrhythms is about expanding your aural perception and being able to perceive 2 different subdivisions of time at the same moment.

Concentrate on the main beat and shift your attention from one subdivision to the other.

In this exercise the only subdivision is in the eighth notes on the 2nd beat of the measure.

Previous Exercise

PTBv1-XY2c3

66

There's a 2 measure pattern. In the first measure of the pattern you are only playing with your **left hand**. The second measure is exactly the same but playing one note with your **right hand**. Try to make them sound rhythmically the same, even though they are different.

This exercise has the **right-hand** note being played an 8ve apart, wich makes it stand out from the pattern. **Pay close attention to where this note lands in the pattern.**

"A jazz musician is a juggler who uses harmonies instead of oranges. " **Benny Green**

mDecks

MP3 download code

Q865L056

Ex. Page Reference

HB-3

X Against Y 3c2

C Position. Preparing 3 against 2

Notes/Comments

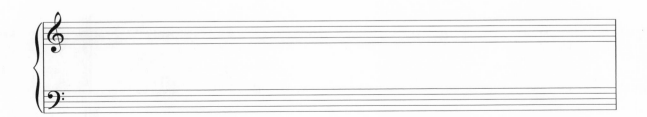

X Against Y 2d3

Place your hands in C Position.

Playing 2 notes against 3 notes and vice versa:
Actually playing 2 against 3 in both hands

mDecks ID:

PTBv1-XY2d3

7 min.

Should be played at all tempos. Metronome from 50 to 140 per quarter note.

Playing Polyrhythms is about expanding your aural perception and being able to perceive 2 different subdivisions of time at the same moment.

Concentrate on the main beat and shift your attention from one subdivision to the other.

Previous Exercise

PTBv1-XY2b3

64

"He who sings scares away his woes. " **Cervantes**

MP3 download code

Q514L464

Ex. Page Reference

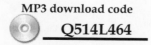

HB-3

X Against Y 2d3

C Position. Same Notes. 2 against 3 against 2

Notes/Comments

Finger Repetitions

X Against Y F32

Place your hands in C Position.

Playing 2 notes against 3 notes and vice versa:

Actually playing 2 against 3 in both hands

mDecks ID:

PTBv1-XYF32

7 min.

Should be played at all tempos. Metronome from 50 to 140 per quarter note.

Playing Polyrhythms is about expanding your aural perception and being able to perceive 2 different subdivisions of time at the same moment.

Concentrate on the main beat and shift your attention from one subdivision to the other.

This exercise is notated exactly as 2vs3 (or 3vs2) so that if you focus on one hand you can hear a pattern of 3 notes and if you focus on the other hand you can hear a pattern of 2 (each with its relative tempo)

Previous Exercise

PTBv1-XY2b3

64

You have to be able to separate, in your mind, the 2 tempos while playing them at the same time. Get rid of all accents and play notes as legatto as possible.

"Music is love in search of a word. " **Sidney Lanier**

MP3 download code

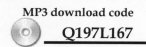
Q197L167

Ex. Page Reference

HB-3

X Against Y F32

C Position. Same Notes. 3 Agianst 2 Final.

Notes/Comments

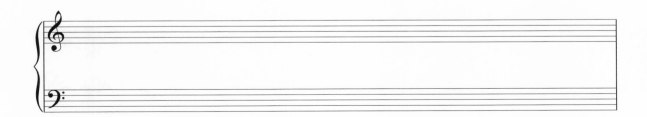

Three Waltzing, Two Singing

Place your hands in C Position.

A little piece in C major with emphasis on 2vs3:

mDecks ID:

PTBv1-SngF23

15 min.

In this piece you'll be playing 3 against 1 in alternation and 3 against 2

Should be played at different tempos. Metronome from 60 to 80 per quarter note.

Playing Polyrhythms is about expanding your aural perception and being able to perceive 2 different subdivisions of time at the same moment.

Concentrate on the main beat and shift your attention from one subdivision to the other.

Previous Exercise

PTBv1-XYF32

74

Carefully play the slurs as indicated to make the shifting clear. On rehearsal mark **A** you start playing 3 against 2. If tou concentrate on your left hand you will be able to hear a new tempo appear.

You have to be able to separate, in your mind, the 2 tempos while playing them at the same time. Get rid of all accents and play notes as legatto as possible.

"Life is one grand, sweet song, so start the music. " **Ronald Reagan**

mDecks

MP3 download code

Q566L522

Ex. Page Reference

HB-3

Three Waltzing, Two Singing

C major Piece

X Against Y 3a4

Place your hands in C Position

mDecks ID:

PTBv1-XY3a4

5 min.

Preparing to play 4 notes against 3 notes:

This is the first exercise for preparing playing the 4 against 3 polyrhythm.

Should be played at all tempos. Metronome from 50 to 160 per quarter note.

Playing Polyrhythms is about expanding your aural perception and being able to perceive 2 different subdivisions of time at the same moment.

Concentrate on the main beat and shift your attention from one subdivision to the other.

In this exercise the only subdivision is in the eighth notes on the 2nd & 4th beats of the measure.

Previous Exercise

PTBv1-XY3a4

78

"Bach opens a vista to the universe. After experiencing him, people feel there is meaning to life after all. "
Helmut Walcha

mDecks

MP3 download code

Q798L564

Ex. Page Reference
HB-3

mDecks.com

78

X Against Y 3a4

C Position. Same Fingers. Preparing 3 against 4

Notes/Comments

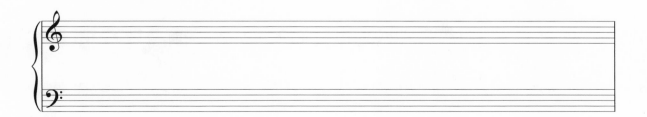

Finger Repetitions

X Against Y 3b4

Place your hands in C Position

Preparing to play 4 notes against 3 notes:
This is the 2nd exercise for preparing playing the 4 against 3 polyrhythm.

Should be played at all tempos. Metronome from 50 to 160 per quarter note.

Playing Polyrhythms is about expanding your aural perception and being able to perceive 2 different subdivisions of time at the same moment.

Concentrate on the main beat and shift your attention from one subdivision to the other.

There's only one eighth note **out of sync**, the rest of the notes are played simultaneously on both hands.

mDecks ID:

PTBv1-XY3b4

5 min.

Previous Exercise

PTBv1-XY3a4

78

"Silence is the fabric upon which the notes are woven. " **Lawrence Duncan**

MP3 download code

Q302L043

Ex. Page Reference

HB-3

mDecks

X Against Y 3b4

C Position. Same Notes. Preparing 3 against 4

Notes/Comments

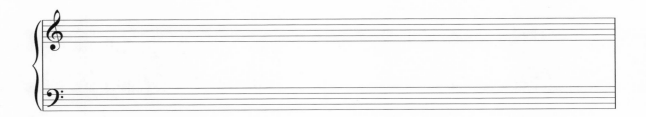

X Against Y 3c4

Place your hands in C Position

mDecks ID:

PTBv1-XY3c4

7 min.

Previous Exercise

PTBv1-XY3b4

80

Preparing to play 4 notes against 3 notes:
Removing upbeats for the 4 vs. 3.

Should be played at all tempos. Metronome from 50 to 180 per quarter note.

Playing Polyrhythms is about expanding your aural perception and being able to perceive 2 different subdivisions of time at the same moment.

Concentrate on the main beat and shift your attention from one subdivision to the other.

This exercise is like 3b4 but removing beats 2 and 4 from the even pattern (making the quarter notes into halfs)

It is important to keep that eighth note (in the & of 2) where it goes. Concentrate on avoiding playing it on the downbeat of the 2nd beat. (Listen to the metronome and remember that eighth plays **after** the 2nd beat)x

"A painter paints pictures on canvas. But musicians paint their pictures on silence." **Leopold Stokowski**

MP3 download code

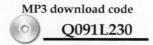

Q091L230

Ex. Page Reference

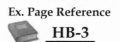

HB-3

X Against Y 3c4

C Position. Pedal Tone. Preparing 3 against 4

Notes/Comments

Finger Repetitions

X Against Y 3d4

Place your hands in C Position

Preparing to play 4 notes against 3 notes:
Removing upbeats and 3rd beat.

mDecks ID:

PTBv1-XY3c4

7 min.

Should be played at all tempos. Metronome from 50 to 180 per quarter note.

Playing Polyrhythms is about expanding your aural perception and being able to perceive 2 different subdivisions of time at the same moment.

Concentrate on the main beat and shift your attention from one subdivision to the other.

This exercise is like 3c4 but removing the 3rd beat of the pattern with the eighth note.

Previous Exercise

PTBv1-XY3c4

82

It is important to keep that eighth note (in the & of 2) where it goes. Concentrate on avoiding playing it on the downbeat of the 2nd beat. (Listen to the metronome and remember that eighth plays **after** the 2nd beat)

Also notice this is **not** a 2 vs 3 polyrhthm (it is not an even 3 pattern)

"Music produces a kind of pleasure which human nature cannot do without. " **Confucius**

mDecks

MP3 download code

Q030L169

Ex. Page Reference

HB-3

X Against Y 3d4

C Position. Pedal Tone. Preparing 3 against 4

Notes/Comments

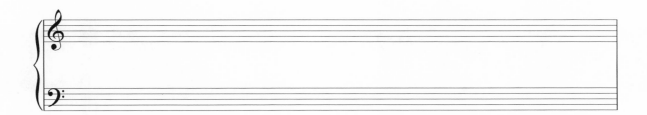

X Against Y 3e4

Place your hands in C Position

Preparing to play 4 notes against 3 notes:

Preparing the 2nd half of the 4 vs. 3 polyrhythm.

mDecks ID:

PTBv1-XY3c4

5 min.

Should be played at all tempos. Metronome from 50 to 180 per quarter note.

Playing Polyrhythms is about expanding your aural perception and being able to perceive 2 different subdivisions of time at the same moment.

Concentrate on the main beat and shift your attention from one subdivision to the other.

This second half of the polyrhythm has another eighth note **out of sync**, in the & of 1.

Previous Exercise

PTBv1-XY3c4

82

This 2 measure pattern makes it easy to play that **"& of 1"** having all the eighth notes played for beats 1 and 2.

Again: *Left hand is accustomed to playing the longer notes. Don't feel disappointed when the tempos become to fast for your left hand to follow since this is very normal.*

"Were it not for music, we might in these days say, the Beautiful is dead. " **Benjamin Disraeli**

MP3 download code

Q361L964

Ex. Page Reference

HB-3

mDecks

X Against Y 3e4

C Position. Pedal Tone. Preparing 3 against 4

Notes/Comments

X Against Y 3f4

Place your hands in C Position

Preparing 3 against 4 combination:

Puting the 2 halfs of the 4 vs. 3 polyrhythm together.

mDecks ID:

PTBv1-XY3f4

5 min.

Should be played at all tempos. Metronome from 50 to 180 per quarter note.

Playing Polyrhythms is about expanding your aural perception and being able to perceive 2 different subdivisions of time at the same moment.

Concentrate on the main beat and shift your attention from one subdivision to the other.

The first part of the polyrhythm has an eighth note in the "& of 2" . The second part of the polyrhythm has another eighth note **out of sync**, in the "& of 5".

Previous Exercise

PTBv1-XY3a4

78

Left hand is playing 3 and right hand is preparing 4.

"It is incontestable that music induces in us a sense of the infinite and the contemplation of the invisible. "
Victor de LaPrade

𝑚𝒟𝑒𝑐𝑘𝑠

MP3 download code

Q134L603

Ex. Page Reference

HB-3

X Against Y 3f4

C Position. Pedal Tone. Preparing 3 against 4 Combination

Notes/Comments

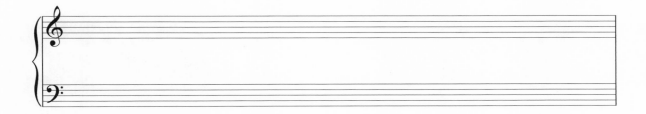

X Against Y 4e3

Place your hands in C Position

Preparing 4 against 3 combination:

Puting the 2 halfs of the 3 vs. 4 polyrhythm together.

mDecks ID:

PTBv1-XY4e3

5 min.

Should be played at all tempos. Metronome from 50 to 180 per quarter note.

Playing Polyrhythms is about expanding your aural perception and being able to perceive 2 different subdivisions of time at the same moment.

Concentrate on the main beat and shift your attention from one subdivision to the other.

Right hand is playing 3 and left hand is preparing 4.

Previous Exercise

PTBv1-XY3a4

78

Left hand is accustomed to playing the longer notes. Don't feel disappointed when the tempos become to fast for your left hand to follow since this is very normal.

mDecks

MP3 download code

Q667L834

Ex. Page Reference

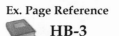

HB-3

X Against Y 4e3

C Position. Pedal Tone. Preparing 4 against 3

Notes/Comments

Finger Repetitions

X Against Y F34

Place your hands in C Position.

mDecks ID:

PTBv1-XYF34

7 min.

Previous Exercise

PTBv1-XY4e3

90

Playing 3 notes against 4 notes and vice versa:

Actually playing 4 against 3 in both hands

Should be played at all tempos. Metronome from 50 to 140 per quarter note.

Playing Polyrhythms is about expanding your aural perception and being able to perceive 2 different subdivisions of time at the same moment.

Concentrate on the main beat and shift your attention from one subdivision to the other.

This exercise is notated exactly as 3vs4 (or 4vs3) so that if you focus on one hand you can hear a pattern of 3 notes and if you focus on the other hand you can hear a pattern of 4 (each with its relative tempo)

You have to be able to separate, in your mind, the 2 tempos while playing them at the same time. Get rid of all accents and play notes as legatto as possible.

"Music is your own experience, your thoughts, your wisdom. If you don't live it, it won't come out of your horn. " **Charlie Parker**

mDecks

MP3 download code

Q587L965

Ex. Page Reference

HB-3

X Against Y F34

C Position. Pedal Tone. 3 against 4 Final

Notes/Comments

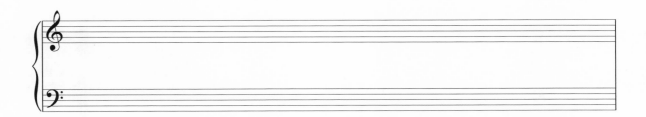

C, 4 Against 3, See?

Place your hands in C Position.

A little piece in C major with emphasis on 4vs3

mDecks ID:

PTBv1-SngF34

15 min.

In this piece you'll be playing 4 against 3 starting in a time signature of 3/2 and finishing with a new tempo (corresponding 4 over that 3/2) of 4/4.

Should be tried at different tempos. Metronome from 120 to 140 per half note.

Playing Polyrhythms is about expanding your aural perception and being able to perceive 2 different subdivisions of time at the same moment.

Concentrate on the main beat and shift your attention from one subdivision to the other.

Previous Exercise

PTBv1-XYF34

92

Carefully play the slurs as indicated to make the shifting clear. On rehearsal mark **B** you should start concentrating on the 4 beat pattern on the right hand and turn it into your new tempo (the metronome should actually feel as being clicking in another tempo). By rehearsal mark **C** you should be in that new tempo.

You have to be able to separate, in your mind, the 2 tempos while playing them at the same time. Get rid of all accents and play notes as legatto as possible.

"Music expresses that which cannot be said and on which it is impossible to be silent. " **Victor Hugo**

mDecks

MP3 download code

Q880L355

Ex. Page Reference

HB-3

C, 4 Against 3, See?

C Major Piece

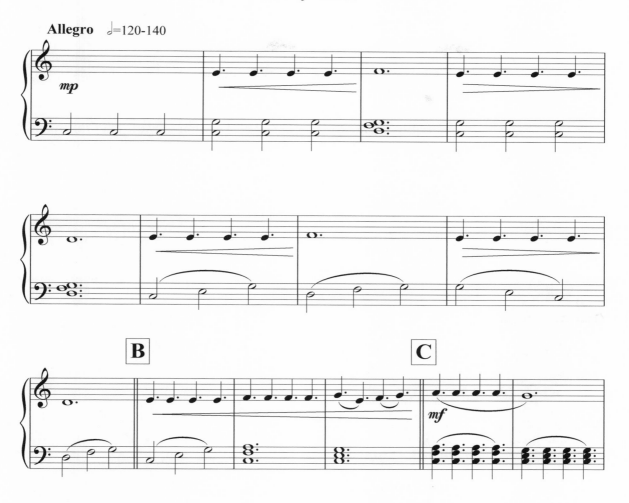

The mDecks Series

1440477647

52 Weeks of Practice

A four topic a week organizing system
for the entire year

This weekly assignment sheets for musicians are essential to established
a consistent system of studies. Each page contain four empty records.
Each record has the necessary fields to keep good track of your practice
habits such as: Title, mDeck Cid , 7 checkable slots for each day of that
week, and a log for comments, progress and reference.

Also each sheet includes a double staff system for additional
writing and explanations.

Common Time

Learning to count rhythms is one of the most important skills any
musician must have. Rhythm is the foundation of Music.
Without Rhythm there is no Music.

OBJECT OF THE GAME

C.T. is a card game for 2, 3 or 4 players where the deck of cards is custom
made with musical symbols instead of numbers and the ordinary suits.
It consists of making tricks of cards that complete a 4/4 measure (3/4 &
more in advanced version). After the decks of cards has been played an
interesting counting of points takes place where strategy and tactics will
determine scoring.

mDecks Books

Many more books and tools are part of the mDecks series.
The mProducts series encompassed a wide range of topics such as: theory,
rhythm, improvisation, technique, music card games, and the focus series.

Check for these and more at **www.mDecks.com**

Made in the USA
San Bernardino, CA
25 January 2015